# VERGHESE KURIEN

Reference Sources:

*I Too Had a Dream*, Verghese Kurien as told to Gouri Salvi; Roli Books
Pvt Ltd, New Delhi. Seventh impression, 2012
and
National Dairy Development Board (NDDB)
http://www.nddb.org/



Comic book design, visual script, cover art, colouring and lettering : Dhruva Rao
Colour script, title design, cover layout and colour: Manasi Parikh



Published by Scholastic India Pvt. Ltd.
A subsidiary of Scholastic Inc., New York, 10012 (USA).
*Publishers since 1920*, with international operations in Canada,
Australia, New Zealand, the United Kingdom, India, and Hong Kong.



For information regarding permission, write to:
Scholastic India Pvt. Ltd.
A-27, Ground Floor, Bharti Sigma Centre
Infocity-1, Sector 34, Gurgaon 122001 (India)

First edition: July 2014

This reprint edition, September 2025

ISBN-13: 978-93-5103-277-9

Printed at Shiv Shakti Printing & Trading Co., Haryana

# VERGHESE KURIEN

## THE MILKMAN OF INDIA

TEXT : ROHINI CHOWDHURY
ART : DHRUVA RAO

**SCHOLASTIC**
New York Toronto London Auckland
Sydney New Delhi Hong Kong

**ROHINI CHOWDHURY** is a widely published children's writer, and an established literary translator. As a children's writer, she has more than twenty books and several short stories to her credit. Her published writing is in Hindi and English, and covers a wide spectrum of literary genres including translations, novels, short fiction, comics, and non-fiction. Her most recent publications for children include *The Garden of the Djinn*, a fantasy adventure novel. Rohini's primary languages as a literary translator are pre-modern (Braj Bhasha and Avadhi) and modern (Khari Boli) Hindi, and English. Her translations include the seventeenth century Braj Bhasha text *Ardhakathanak*, widely regarded as the first autobiography in an Indian language, into modern Hindi and into English, and the Hindi novel *Tyagpatra* [*The Resignation*] by Jainendra, one of the leading Hindi novelists of the modern period, into English. Rohini also runs a story website at www.longlongtimeago.com.

**DHRUVA RAO** is an illustrator and dinosaur activist who has yet to realise the redundancy of both his career choices. Go Stego!

**MANASI PARIKH** is a junior dinosaur activist with a natural flair for disaster management.

With a unique mix of text and the comic book format, the new **SCHOLASTIC BIOGRAPHIES SERIES** captures the **'GREAT LIVES'** that have inspired generations and continue to motivate young and old alike.

Forthcoming titles in this series:

Amrita Sher-Gil

Mahatma Gandhi

MC Mary Kom

Ravi Shankar

Sachin Tendulkar

And many others.

ANAND JUNCTION

# CHAPTER ONE

# 'BEGINNINGS'

IT WAS FRIDAY, MAY 13, 1949, WHEN A YOUNG MAN CALLED VERGHESE KURIEN ARRIVED IN THE SMALL, SLEEPY LITTLE TOWN OF ANAND IN GUJARAT.
ANAND JUNCTION
આણંદ જંક્શન
आणंद जंक्शन

HE HAD BEEN SENT BY THE GOVERNMENT OF INDIA TO BE THE NEW DAIRY ENGINEER AT THE GOVERNMENT RESEARCH CREAMERY THERE.

KURIEN DID NOT WANT THE JOB.

UT THE GOVERNMENT HAD PAID
OR HIS EDUCATION IN THE USA...

...AND HE WAS UNDER CONTRACT
TO THEM TO WORK WHEREVER
THEY SENT HIM.

ANAND JUNCTION

T FIRST GLANCE, THERE COULD
AVE BEEN NO ONE MORE
NSUITED TO THE POST THAN
URIEN.

THROW

N ENGINEER WITH A PASSION
OR METALLURGY AND PHYSICS,

HE HAD BEEN FORCED TO STUDY
DAIRY ENGINEERING,

AND HAD LITTLE KNOWLEDGE OF
AGRICULTURE OR DAIRY
FARMING.
CLANG!

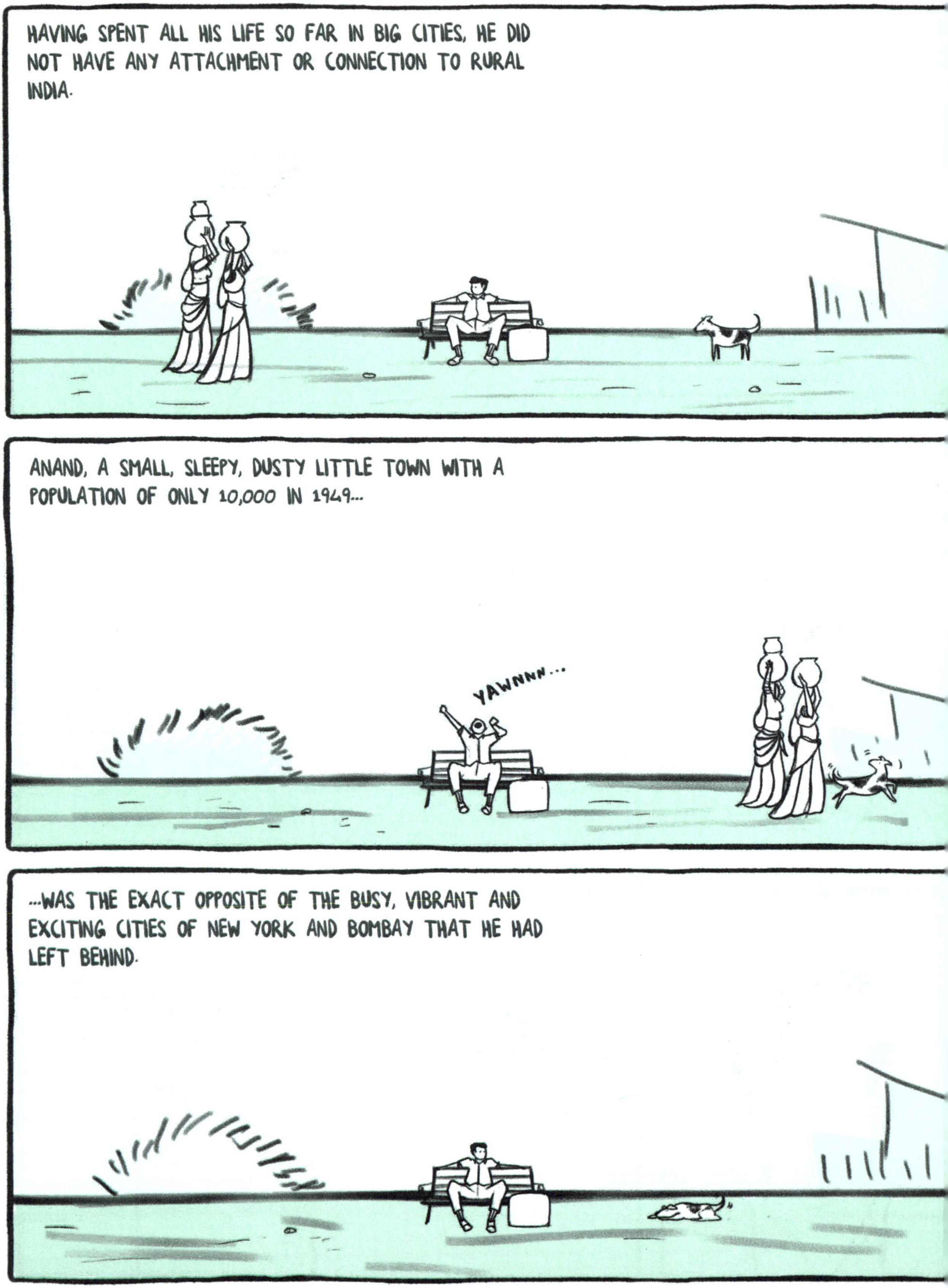

HAVING SPENT ALL HIS LIFE SO FAR IN BIG CITIES, HE DID NOT HAVE ANY ATTACHMENT OR CONNECTION TO RURAL INDIA.

ANAND, A SMALL, SLEEPY, DUSTY LITTLE TOWN WITH A POPULATION OF ONLY 10,000 IN 1949...



...WAS THE EXACT OPPOSITE OF THE BUSY, VIBRANT AND EXCITING CITIES OF NEW YORK AND BOMBAY THAT HE HAD LEFT BEHIND.

E HAD COME TO ANAND UNDER
URESS,

AND HE WAS DETERMINED TO
FIND HIS WAY OUT AGAIN AS
QUICKLY AS POSSIBLE.

ITTLE DID HE KNOW THAT HE WAS TO FIND HIS LIFE'S WORK HERE,

ORK THAT WOULD TRANSFORM INDIA'S DAIRY INDUSTRY, AND WITH
T, THE LIVES OF HUNDREDS OF THOUSANDS OF HER FARMERS.

He was born, the third of four children, on November 26, 1921, in the city of Kozhikode, in the southern Indian state of Kerala. His parents named him 'Verghese' after his uncle, Rao Saheb P.K. Verghese, an important man in the town of Ernakulam. His father, Puthenparakkal Kurien, was a civil surgeon in Cochin. His mother was a talented pianist and belonged to a wealthy and distinguished family of Kerala.

The Kuriens were Syrian Christians and very devout. As a child, the young Verghese was expected to attend Church with the rest of his family, and forced to memorise parts of the Bible. These, and other rituals, turned him away from religion, so that he became and remained an atheist all his life.

The Syrian Christian community was highly literate and placed great emphasis on education. Academically gifted, Verghese Kurien joined Loyola College, Madras, to study science, at the very young age of fourteen. He graduated at the age of nineteen but, still too young to join an engineering college, did an extra degree in Physics at Loyola College. He then joined Guindy College of Engineering in Madras. Verghese Kurien was not only an exceptional student, but also passionate about sports—a passion he had inherited from his father who had been somewhat of an athlete as a young man and had been known as 'Hundred-yard dash Kurien'. Verghese represented his college in tennis, badminton, cricket and boxing.

While in college, he also joined the University Training Corps (UTC), an organisation that had been set up by the British government to impart military training to young people in India, and which later became the National Cadet Corps. Interestingly, the officer in command of his battalion was one Captain K.S. Thimmaiah, who later went on to become the Chief of Army Staff of independent India. Young Kurien distinguished himself in the UTC as much as he did in academics, and was selected as the best cadet of his battalion. He loved the discipline of the UTC and the perfection it demanded so much that he began to consider the army a serious career option. But before he could make up his mind, his father suddenly and unexpectedly died. His mother's family, which was as close-knit as it was influential, stepped in to provide both economic and emotional support. Kurien's great-uncle, Cherian Matthai, took him, along with his siblings and their mother, to live with him in Thrissur.

Fondly known as 'Master Matthai' in the Syrian Christian community, Cherian Matthai had never married. He was also the head of the family and very much the patriarch, taking it upon himself to look after everyone, even sending his brothers and sister to England to study. Even before their father died, the Kurien children used to spend their summer holidays with Cherian Matthai, who 'lived in a sprawling house upon a hundred-acre estate', complete with 'a boat club, gymnasium, golf course and excellent cooks'. His large and beautiful house now became the home of the Kurien family.

Kurien soon graduated with a B.E. in Mechanical Engineering from Guindy. Meanwhile, his mother succeeded in dissuading him from joining the army, and urged him to apply to TISCO, the Tata Iron and Steel Company (which is the multinational Tata Steel today), instead. Kurien gave in, and in 1944, applied to TISCO for an apprenticeship.

TISCO had been established by the Tatas in 1907, and by 1939, it operated the largest steel plant in the British Empire. The post of Graduate Apprentice in TISCO was an extremely coveted position at the time, for the company selected only ten such apprentices in a year.

Now, another family member stepped in to help. This was John Matthai, the younger brother of Cherian Matthai. He was almost the same age as Kurien's mother, and more a brother to her than an uncle. He was also the Director of Tata Industries, and took it upon himself to recommend his young nephew to the then Managing Director of TISCO, Jehangir Ghandy, asking him to consider his application 'if found competent'. Since John Matthai was Ghandy's superior, the latter could not refuse his request, and Verghese Kurien was taken on by TISCO as a Graduate Apprentice and sent to Jamshedpur, to the company's steel plant there.

Though Kurien accepted the post and moved to Jamshedpur, he was very unhappy that his uncle had recommended him. He was sure he would have got in on his own merit, had he been allowed to do so. One day, John Matthai visited Kurien in the hostel in Jamshedpur where he lived with the other apprentices. This made matters much worse, for the other apprentices recognised John Matthai, and discovering Kurien's relationship with him, became convinced that Kurien was slated for special favours and a rapid rise to the top in the company. Kurien found this state of affairs unbearable. He decided to leave TISCO and applied for a government scholarship to study abroad for a Master's degree in Metallurgy and Nuclear Physics.

John Matthai was deeply disapproving of his nephew's decision, which he declared to be 'very, very commendable, but also extremely stupid,' for, said he, Kurien was regarded as the best among the apprentices and was sure to do very well. But Kurien was adamant. Fortunately for him, the government scholarship selection committee called him for an interview.

The interview and its outcome can best be described in Kurien's own words. As he tells us in his autobiography:

… the chairman of the selection committee, after inviting me to sit down, asked me only one question.

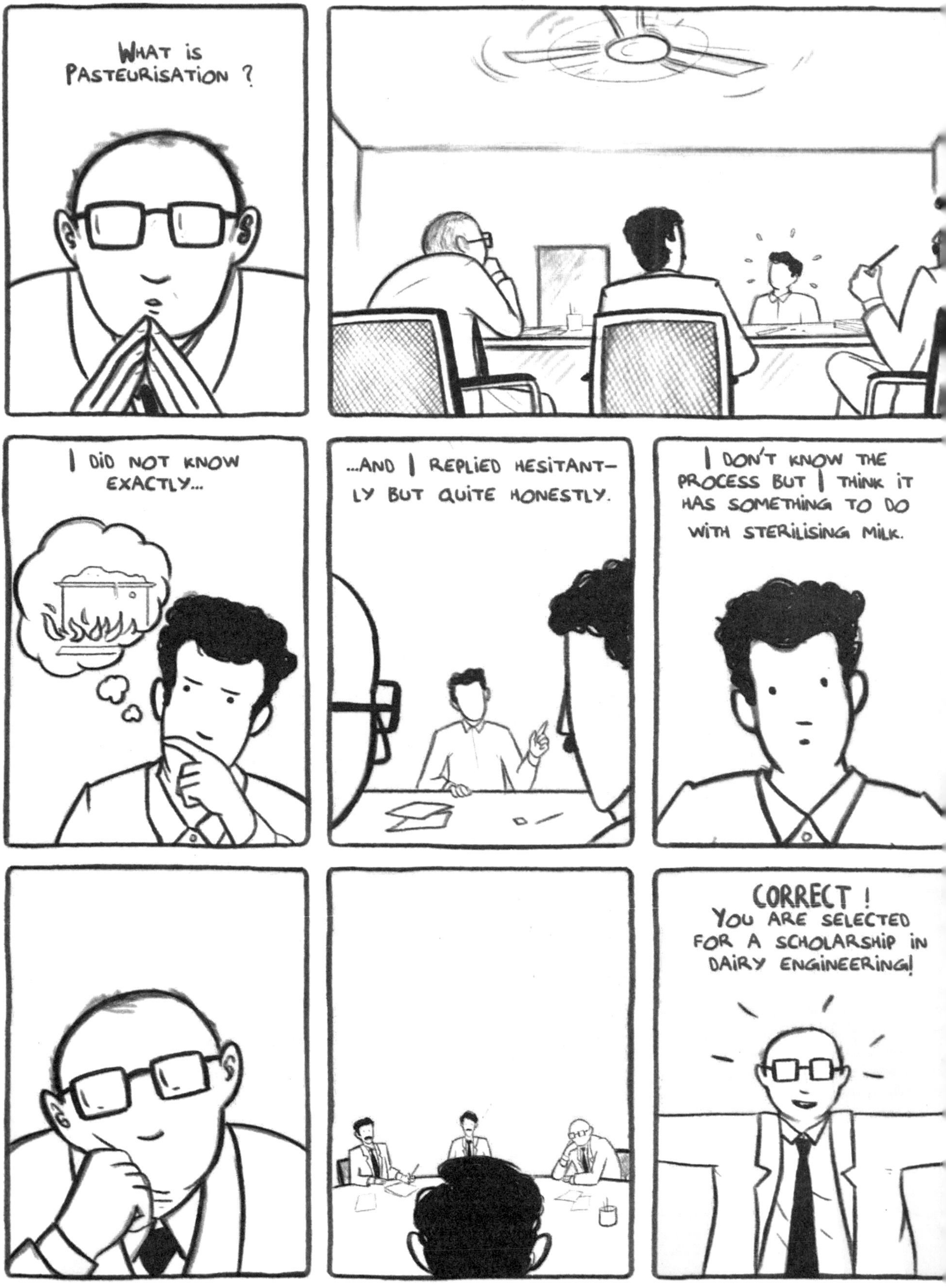

WHAT IS PASTEURISATION ?

I DID NOT KNOW EXACTLY...

...AND I REPLIED HESITANTLY BUT QUITE HONESTLY.

DAIRY ENGINEERING!

DAIRY ENGINEERING!

CAN'T YOU GIVE ME METALLURGY OR NUCLEAR PHYSICS ?

NO. IT'S EITHER THIS OR NOTHING,

MAKE UP YOUR MIND.

KURIEN KNEW NOTHING ABOUT DAIRY ENGINEERING,

OR WAS HE AT ALL
TERESTED IN THE FIELD.

BUT HE WAS ABSOLUTELY CLEAR THAT HE DID NOT WISH TO WORK FOR TISCO ANYMORE...

...AND SO HE ACCEPTED THE SCHOLARSHIP TO GO TO THE USA AND STUDY TO BECOME A DAIRY ENGINEER.

The government first sent him to Bangalore, to the Imperial Dairy Research Institute (which later became the National Dairy Research Institute of India), so that he could become familiar with the basic principles of dairying. From the very first day, Kurien disliked being at the institute. The others looked upon him as an outsider, someone who knew nothing about dairy, yet had been given a prestigious scholarship by the government. The teachers were not interested in him, and one of them, Kodandapani, took an instant dislike to him. But it was too late for Kurien to go back on his decision now, and he had to make the best of where he found himself. Luckily for Kurien, it was not all bad: he made friends with two dairy technologists there, A.T. Dudani and Pheroze Medora. Their company made life at the institute a little more bearable for Kurien. As far as Kurien was concerned, the eight months in Bangalore were a complete waste of time for him. He could not wait to get his scholarship and leave for the USA.

It was finally in the winter of 1946 that Kurien left for the USA, to study at Michigan State University, considered at that time to be the best for dairy engineering. But the world was changing—the first atomic bomb had been exploded only the previous year over Japan, finally bringing an end to the Second World War, and nuclear physics was the new excitement in the academic world. Kurien decided to follow his dream. Except for a few token courses to satisfy the Government of India, he abandoned dairy engineering and took up metallurgy and nuclear physics.

Soon after, Kurien's friend from Bangalore, Medora, also joined the university. So did another young man called Harichand Dalaya. Medora and Dalaya were already friends since they had been together in college, and soon Dalaya became a close friend of Kurien's as well. Several years later, the three men were to become close associates in bringing about India's dairy revolution.

Kurien thoroughly enjoyed his years at Michigan State University. Inherently brilliant, he more than fulfilled the academic requirements of the university with ease, with enough time left over for tennis and other interests. Of course, he continued to ignore dairy engineering, and pursued his interest in metallurgy, choosing to study the properties of cast iron for his research project. During his research, Kurien, working with his professor, made the exciting discovery that cast iron, like steel, also had the ability to stretch. This discovery could have made millionaires of Kurien and his professor—but it was not to be, for someone else had already made the discovery before them! Years later, Kurien looked back on this incident. 'Perhaps it was just as well,' he reflected, 'for if I had become a millionaire, I would not have left the US'—and this story may never have been written.

IN 1948, ARMED WITH A MASTER'S DEGREE IN METALLURGY AND NUCLEAR PHYSICS...

...KURIEN RETURNED HOME.

INDIA, NEWLY INDEPENDENT AND DEEPLY SCARRED BY PARTITION AND ITS AFTERMATH, WAS IN SORE NEED OF REBUILDING AND RESTRUCTURING.
?

?

?

?

KURIEN'S UNCLE, JOHN MATTHAI, WAS NOW FINANCE MINISTER OF INDIA...
REFUGEES...

...AND KURIEN WENT TO STAY WITH HIM IN DELHI.

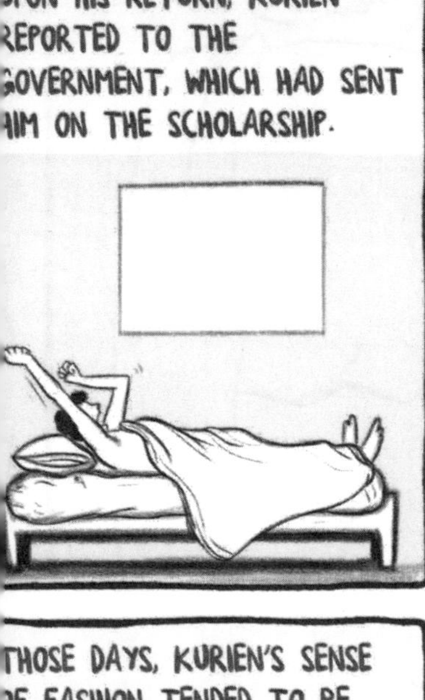
UPON HIS RETURN, KURIEN REPORTED TO THE GOVERNMENT, WHICH HAD SENT HIM ON THE SCHOLARSHIP.

HE WAS TOLD TO GET IN TOUCH WITH THE MINISTRY OF EDUCATION.

HE DID SO, AND WENT ONE MORNING TO SEE THE UNDER SECRETARY, EDUCATION.

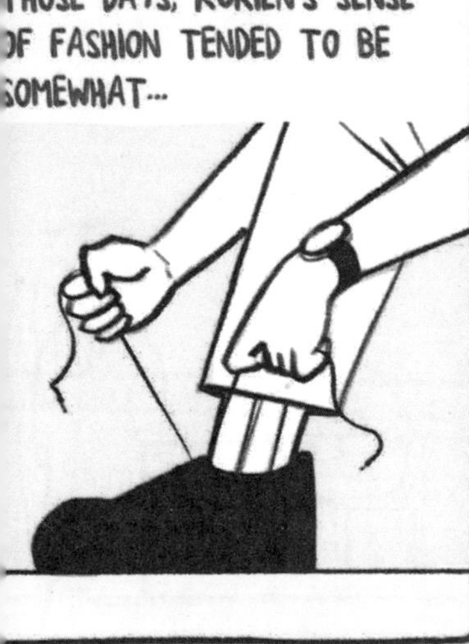
THOSE DAYS, KURIEN'S SENSE OF FASHION TENDED TO BE SOMEWHAT...

...FLAMBOYANT...

HIS FAVOURITE OUTFIT WAS A GREEN SHIRT...

...YELLOW TROUSERS...

...AND A GREEN FELT HAT.
KURIEN ?

AND THIS IS WHAT HE CHOSE TO WEAR ON HIS VISIT TO THE UNDER SECRETARY.

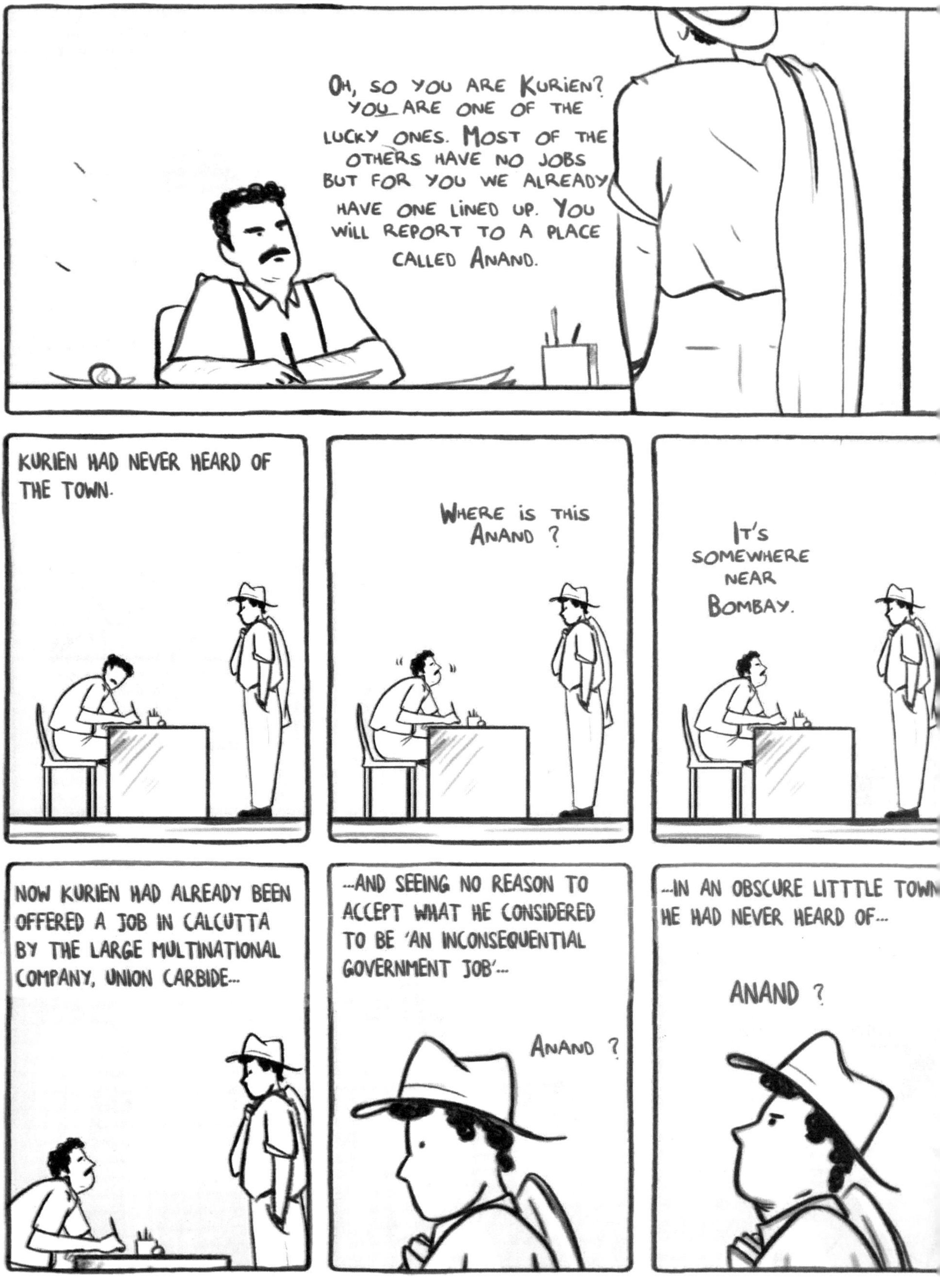

OH, SO YOU ARE KURIEN? YOU ARE ONE OF THE LUCKY ONES. MOST OF THE OTHERS HAVE NO JOBS BUT FOR YOU WE ALREADY HAVE ONE LINED UP. YOU WILL REPORT TO A PLACE CALLED ANAND.

...HE REFUSED.
I'M SORRY, BUT I DON'T THINK I'LL BE TAKING UP THIS POSITION.

THE UNDER SECRETARY, ALREADY IRRITATED BY KURIEN'S OUTFIT AND CASUAL ARROGANCE...

...BECAME EVEN MORE ANNOYED.

HOW CAN YOU TALK LIKE THIS ?

I WILL SUE YOU FOR THE Rs 30,000 THAT WE SPENT ON YOUR HIGHER EDUCATION IF YOU REFUSE TO TAKE UP THIS JOB AT ANAND.

30,000 !!!

IN THOSE DAYS, Rs 30,000 WAS A HUGE SUM OF MONEY...
...AND KURIEN KNEW HE WOULD NEVER BE ABLE TO PAY THAT BACK ON HIS OWN.
HE REALISED HE HAD NO OPTIO BUT TO ACCEPT THE JOB AT ANAND.
FINE, I ACCEPT.
GOOD, WAIT WHILE I WRITE OUT YOUR APPOINTMENT LETTER.
UMM, ACTUALLY...
I DON'T THINK I NEED IT... AND BESIDES...
I PROMISED MY AUNT I'D BE HOME FOR LUNCH.
...
YOUNG MAN, YOU WILL NOT GO TOO FAR IN LIFE, THERE'S NO DOUBT ABOUT THAT !
THOUGH NEITHER HE NOR KURIEN KNEW IT AT THE TIME...
...THE UNDER SECRETARY COULD NOT HAVE BEEN MORE WRONG!

Kurien returned home, and desperate to get out of the job at Anand, asked his uncle, John Matthai, for help. But uncle and nephew were made of the same metal, and John Matthai refused. 'I told you not to leave the Tatas. I told you not to take the government scholarship. You rejected my advice. You wanted to build your future with your own efforts,' he pointed out. 'So go build your future. I will not help you. You have made your bed, my boy. Now go lie in it.' Kurien could not deny the justice of this, and resigned himself to a gloomy existence in Anand.

It did not help when he came to know later that he had initially been chosen for a job as a dairy engineer at the Imperial Dairy Research Institute in Bangalore, a far better job than what he had been given at Anand—it came with a higher salary, and was located in a big city. The officers at the dairy department had not considered Kurien competent enough, and had therefore decided to send him to Anand, and move his old enemy, the less qualified Kodandapani, from Anand to Bangalore. This had irked Kurien greatly at the time, but, many years later, when he looked back on his life at Anand, he felt that had he been given the 'better' job, he might never have achieved what he did. Others, including Kodandapani, had held the same job before him at Anand, but all of them had seen only the boredom and the despair there; it took a man of Kurien's steel to see the challenges and the opportunity that was Anand, and turn it into a success story that shook the world.

CHAPTER TWO
'ANAND'

Kurien was met at the railway station in Anand by Kodandapani, who could now hand over charge of the dilapidated old government creamery to Kurien and return to the more prestigious post at the institute in Bangalore. Though Kodandapani was keen to hand over charge to Kurien, he advised him to wait a day to take over, since Friday the 13th was an inauspicious day to begin a new venture. But Kurien refused to wait, and insisted he would take charge at once. 'No,' he said to Kodandapani, 'I don't like what I see here. Let me take charge today and allow things to go wrong. I'm not interested in staying here too long.' Kodandapani did not protest, and disappeared to Bangalore—and permanent obscurity from these pages—as soon as he could.

Kurien, meanwhile, turned to the task at hand, and found matters to be far worse than he had expected. The government research creamery actually did no research at all. Instead, its purpose was to manufacture milk powder from buffalo milk. But when Kurien took over as dairy engineer, he realised that the creamery was not fulfilling even this simple function.

THE CREAMERY WAS FITTED WITH TWO ROLLER DRYERS USED TO DRY MILK INTO POWDER.
THESE WERE NOT WORKING.
AND THEREFORE NO MILK POWDER WAS BEING PRODUCED
DOWN
THE STAFF—TWENTY MEN EMPLOYED BY THE GOVERNMENT TO RUN THE DRYERS, A JOB THAT COULD HAVE BEEN DONE BY ONE MAN ALONE—WAS UNDEREMPLOYED, BORED AND APATHETIC.
THE SUPERVISOR WAS LAZY AN
UNINTERESTED.
ZZZZ
NO ONE AT THE CREAMERY COULD BE BOTHERED TO FIND OUT WHY THE DRYERS WERE NOT WORKING.
IT TOOK KURIEN ONLY TEN MINUTES TO LOCATE THE PROBLEM AND REPAIR IT.
AND ONCE THE DRYERS WERE RUNNING, PRODUCING MILK POWDER WAS NOT A BIG TASK IN ITSELF.
DOWN

Life in Anand posed its own, unique set of challenges for Kurien. The people of Anand, conservative and close-minded in the extreme, regarded Kurien with horror. He was an alien, an outsider from Kerala, and a Christian, a non-vegetarian and unmarried at that! Their conventional, Gujarati, strictly Hindu and vegetarian ethos did not permit them to even rent him a room. Finally, after days of searching, he managed to rent a rundown old garage to live in.

Determinedly, Kurien turned the derelict garage into a home. He describes his efforts in his autobiography: *The garage had a large, greasy pit in the middle, where mechanics must have once stood to tinker with the undersides of cars. But I was an engineer, and I could not allow such things to get in the way of basic comfort. I filled up the pit. There were no windows, so I created them. There was no bathroom so I put up three corrugated sheets and a makeshift bathroom was ready.*

Initially, to ease the excruciating boredom of life in Anand, Kurien would also make frequent trips to Bombay, where he would stay at the luxurious Taj Hotel, and treat himself to a few days of comfort. His older brother also helped to ease life in Anand—by sending him Anthony, his trained cook and butler. Anthony brought with him a whiff of the life that Kurien had been used to. *Every evening without fail, at dinnertime* [writes Kurien], *Anthony appeared before me in my tiny garage like a genie from Aladdin's lamp. He would be dressed in his impeccable white uniform, with a sash and a turban perfectly in place, fix me with an unwavering look, and announce in all seriousness: 'Master, dinner is served.' And, indeed, my small table would be flawlessly set in one corner of the derelict garage.'* Anthony stayed with Kurien for many years at Anand, bringing elegance and not a little humour into his life there.

This was the beginning of life in Anand for Kurien, full of apparently impossible problems, and quite devoid of the comforts and privileges he had been used to earlier. Despite his unhappiness with the situation, Kurien met the challenges head on. It was perhaps this spirit of never-say-die, together with his tenacity and perseverance, which enabled Kurien to create a miracle where there had never been hope of one.

Back at the creamery, the roller-dryers worked perfectly and milk-powder production continued steadily. Now another problem presented itself—what should be done with the growing stock of milk powder? The supervisor was certain that no one would want to buy it, but Kurien was not convinced, and on one of his trips to Bombay, he approached a biscuit manufacturer and sold him all of the five tonnes of the milk powder they had in stock.

Kurien's success at selling the milk powder merely increased his frustration with his job. It was dull, boring and soul-destroying. He had hardly any work to occupy him or, he felt, to justify the handsome salary of Rs 350 a month that he was drawing. He began to smoke heavily and, discarding his stylish clothes, took to hanging about in his work overalls all day. He spent most of his evening playing cards. Fed up and angry, he began writing to the Ministry of Agriculture in Delhi every month, asking to be released.

But Verghese Kurien was not a man to stay down or idle for too long. While he waited for the Ministry to reply to his letters, he began to look around for something to do with his time. And, as luck would have it, he found Tribhuvandas Patel and the dairy farmers of the Kaira Cooperative Union.

# CHAPTER THREE

# 'COOPERATION AND COOPERATIVES'

The story of Verghese Kurien now becomes the story of the dairy farmers of Gujarat. It is therefore worth pausing at this stage to understand better the origin of the cooperative movement in India, and specifically, the beginnings of the Kaira Cooperative Union.

In 1947, India became an independent nation, finally throwing off some two hundred years of colonial domination and misrule by the British. With Independence also came Partition, as the country was divided into two with the creation of Pakistan. Therefore, in 1949, when Kurien was sent to Anand, India was still a brand-new nation, facing a host of challenges, including the urgent need to feed a large[1] and growing population, increase incomes and provide employment.

At that time, though 83 per cent of India's population lived in villages and was dependent on agriculture for their livelihood, agricultural productivity was very low, and since farm incomes are dependent on production, India's farmers were amongst the poorest in the country.

Indian agriculture suffered from various problems that would have to be addressed if agricultural productivity were to increase. First, only 15 per cent of the land under cultivation had any form of irrigation available. As a result, agriculture became overly dependent on the monsoons,

---

[1] 345 million in 1951

so that even a single year of low rainfall could result in intense shortages and famine. Though there were pockets of prosperity where water was abundant, the lack of irrigation in most areas made production of crops difficult. Farmers, to supplement their income from the land, therefore took up allied activities such as animal husbandry and dairy farming.

Dairy farming was, and still remains, a small, but important sub-sector of agriculture in India. Most farmers own a cow or a buffalo along with their land. The animal is looked after by the women, who sell its milk to supplement the household income. The cow or buffalo is usually regarded as belonging to the farmer's wife, and any income she derives from it is regarded as her income, and comes directly into her hands. But here too, productivity was very low, with a cow or buffalo producing only three to four litres of milk a day, while in countries that had advanced dairy farming techniques, a cow produced 40 litres of milk a day.

Then, the size of the land held by each farmer was very small. Apart from reducing the yield per farmer to very small amounts, this also made it impossible for them to use modern machinery such as tractors to help plough, sow and harvest. Some of the holdings were so tiny that it was not possible to turn a bullock-cart around in one, much less a tractor. The farmers were therefore prevented from the use of modern technology to increase crop yield.

Most farmers need cash to pay for seeds, fertilisers, and sometimes even for labourers to work on their fields. They usually need to borrow to meet these needs. The farmers in India had no credit facility to borrow from banks and other financial institutions. They were dependent on local moneylenders, who charged exorbitant rates of interest and who would often reduce them to the status of landless labourers by taking away their land if the farmers could not repay the loan.

Also, there was no infrastructure in the form of good roads, or trucks and lorries available to them to transport their produce to bigger markets in the cities where they could get a fair price. Therefore they did not get an adequate return on their labour and farm produce. What's more, since they had no access to the bigger markets, they had no information on the markets either, and so did not know when they were being exploited by middlemen and local village landlords, who would buy their produce at ridiculously low prices.

In 1947, India was a net importer of food grains, milk and dairy products, all of which were extremely critical in the Indian diet. It was clear that agricultural productivity had to be increased for the benefit of the nation. In Russia, cooperative farming had been implemented with great success, and the government of the newly-independent India believed that cooperatives would solve most of the problems of India's agricultural sector.

A cooperative worked by bringing together small farmers to work together as a larger unit and, by pooling their resources, helping them to get the advantages and benefits of large-scale production. For example, several farmers could get together and buy a tractor, and use that to plough their small, individual holdings as though they were one big unit. A small farmer could not hope to buy a tractor on his own, or run it on his tiny piece of land. In the case of dairy farmers, milk produced in individual households was too little to be of any significant commercial value. But if the farmers pooled their milk production, then the total production from several households, or a village, could be sold to a dairy for further processing and sale.

In 1949, while Kurien was struggling with his mind-numbingly boring job at the government research creamery, a group of dairy farmers from the neighbouring district of Kaira had set up a small, milk-producers' cooperative. Despite support from the government of India, cooperatives were still considered a bold move by farmers, challenging the authority of local landlords and vested interests, as well as the established systems of production, distribution and sales of agricultural produce.

# THE STORY OF OLSON'S

FOR MANY YEARS, THE MILK BUSINESS IN KAIRA DISTRICT HAD BEEN CONTROLLED AND DOMINATED BY A PARSI GENTLEMAN NAMED PESTONJI EDULJI DALAL.

IN 1888, WHEN HE WAS JUST THIRTEEN YEARS OLD, PESTONJI SET UP A SMALL SHOP SELLING ROASTED AND GROUND COFFEE.

HE WAS KNOWN AS POLLY.

NICKNAME THAT HE QUICKLY MODIFIED TO POLSON AND CLEVERLY USED AS HIS BRAND NAME.

THE ENGLISH-SOUNDING NAME ATTRACTED REGULAR CUSTOMERS FROM THE BRITISH.

AND BY 1910, POLSON'S COFFEE WAS A WELL-ESTABLISHED BUSINESS IN THE REGION.

E THEN SET UP A BUTTER FACTORY TO SUPPLY BUTTER INITIALLY TO BRITISH TROOPS, AND SOLD IT AS POLSON'S BUTTER.

BY 1930, POLSON'S HAD THE MOST ADVANCED DAIRY PLANT IN INDIA,

AND POLSON'S BUTTER BECAME THE MOST POPULAR BRAND OF BUTTER IN INDIA.

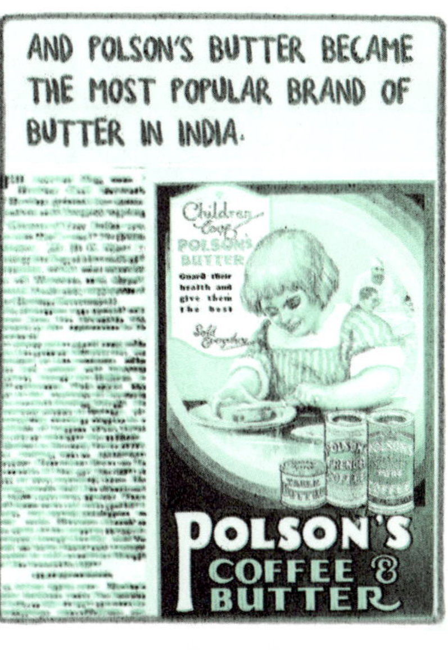

In 1943, several of the British in Bombay fell ill thanks to the poor quality of milk they were drinking. The British government then set up a milk department under a milk commissioner to improve the quality of milk coming into Bombay. In order to accomplish this, the milk department needed to source good quality milk, and very soon their attention was drawn to Kaira district. In addition to Polson's, Kaira also had a butter factory and a casein factory, the first set up and run by an Englishman, and the second by a German. The presence of these three manufacturing units created a demand for liquid milk in the district, to which the dairy farmers of Kaira responded by increasing their milk production. This made Kaira one of the highest milk-producing districts near Bombay. So it was inevitable that the milk department would turn to Kaira. The British government asked Polson's whether it would be able to transport liquid milk to Bombay, a distance of 350 kilometres from Anand.

Those were the days before refrigerated tankers and trains, but Pestonji grabbed the opportunity with both hands. He pasteurised the milk, and sent it to Bombay in milk cans wrapped in sacks soaked in chilled water. The milk arrived reasonably fresh, so that Bombay now provided a market not just for milk products from Kaira, but also for liquid milk. This increase in demand motivated the dairy farmers of Kaira to increase their production of milk even further. This was the beginning of the Bombay Milk Scheme (BMS).

Pestonji, pleased with this success, demanded a processing charge from the government as well as additional equipment, both of which he was given. He also demanded that the government pass a law that no one except him could collect from the villages around Anand. This, too, the government did, with the result that the dairy farmers now had to sell all their milk to the milk contractors chosen by Polson.

This arrangement ensured that Bombay received its supply of good quality, fresh milk; at the same time, Polson's business increased, and so did that of the milk contractors. The only people to suffer were the dairy farmers, since no one except Polson was allowed to collect milk in the region, they had no choice but to sell to Polson's contractors, and at the price they offered. Though the government offered Polson a much higher price for the milk it supplied, almost all of this increase was shared between Polson and his milk contractors. The dairy farmers received only a very tiny part of it. So the dairy farmers took their complaint to Sardar Vallabhbhai Patel.

Sardar Patel, prominent in India's fight for independence from the British, and soon to become the Deputy Prime Minister of independent India, came from the village of Karamsad, near Anand. A firm believer in teamwork, he advised the farmers to form milk cooperatives, which, he felt, was the only way they could gain control over both the production and distribution of milk and keep the income that they generated. He deputed Morarji Desai to help the farmers organise themselves. Morarjibhai was his junior and another freedom fighter; he later became the fourth Prime Minister of India.

At a meeting of the dairy farmers, Morarjibhai chose a young man named Tribhuvandas Kishibhai Patel to lead the farmers as chairman of the Kaira milk cooperatives. Tribhuvandas Patel was also a follower of Sardar Patel, and his dedicated participation in India's freedom struggle had led him to be imprisoned by the British several times.

Tribhuvandas Patel did not want to be the chairman. 'I've just come out of jail for the fourth time and my health is not so good. I just want to go home and recover. Besides, I don't know anything about the dairy business,' he protested. But his very desire *not* to be chairman made him the perfect choice, because, reasoned Morarji Desai, his refusal indicated that he had no vested interest at all. And so Tribhuvandas Patel became the chairman of the Kaira Cooperatives.

It was relatively easy to form cooperatives, but not so easy to battle Polson, who still remained the sole buyer of milk in the region. Given that milk is so perishable, the dairy farmers did not have the option of taking it anywhere further to sell, for it would spoil by the time they reached there. Polson did not like the cooperatives, and made it as difficult for them as possible. He would manufacture excuses to reject their milk or pay them less—there were flies in the milk, the fat content was too low, the milk smelled strange, and so on. Harassed and at their wits' end, Tribhuvandas and the farmers once again took their problems to Sardar Patel.

His advice was simple—throw out Polson, which in practical terms meant breaking the unfair legislation passed by the British government that gave Polson the power and special privileges he enjoyed. Sardar Patel explained that the only way they could hope to get a fair deal was to cooperatise the dairy business completely and for them to own a dairy. It was now 1945—India was still fighting for independence from British rule. Sardar Patel warned the farmers that their struggle against exploitation would be viewed by the government as a political, anti-British move, even though it was not, and they should be prepared for stiff opposition. 'But,' he added, 'if you are prepared to struggle, to bear the losses, to fight the milk commissioner of Bombay and his department, then I am prepared to lead you.'

The farmers agreed, and thus began the cooperative dairy movement in Kaira, a farmers' initiative against the British government.

In January 1946, Morarji Desai came to Kaira, and held a meeting of the dairy farmers under a banyan tree in Chaklashi village, a few kilometres from Anand. Only two resolutions were passed at the meeting: first, that the dairy farmers would not sell their milk to Polson, and second, they would create a cooperative in each village of Kaira district, and a union of these cooperatives in Anand, which would handle the processing of milk, thus giving the farmers control over the procurement, processing and marketing of their milk.

Morarji Desai then demanded that the BMS buy milk directly from the farmers' cooperatives, and not from Polson's dairy. Of course, the demand was rejected. In response, the dairy farmers went on strike. They refused to sell their milk to Polson, pouring it on to the streets instead. Polson could no longer collect milk and supply it to Bombay, and the BMS, which relied heavily on Polson, collapsed.

The milk commissioner of Bombay decided to visit Anand. He was accompanied by his deputy, another Parsi gentleman called Dara Khurody. When they saw that the farmers were not willing to move from their stand, Khurody advised the milk commissioner to give in to their demands. 'Look at their leader Tribhuvandas Patel. He wears a Gandhi topi, he cannot speak English. How is he going to handle this milk business? This is not New Zealand or Denmark. This is India. Milk business is a technical thing. Do you really think the cooperatives in Anand can succeed? Concede to their demands; they are only doomed to failure,' he said. (Of course, it is another matter that later Khurody went on to set up the 3,200-acre Aarey Milk Colony in Bombay, which became the largest state-owned, milk-producing centre in the world, and the model for similar colonies in Calcutta and Chennai.)

The Milk Commissioner did as Khurody advised, and gave in to the demands of the dairy farmers. That was all the impetus Tribhuvandas Patel needed. He spent the rest of the year spreading the message of cooperatives in the villages of Kaira district so that, by the end of 1946, five cooperative societies had been formed, and the Kaira District Cooperative Milk Producers Union Limited (KDCMPUL) was registered at Anand.

The following year, 1947, India became independent, and Sardar Patel the country's Deputy Prime Minister. Tribhuvandas Patel went to Delhi to meet him, and asked for the use of an old creamery in Anand, that had been built in 1914, but had fallen into disuse. This had been acquired by the National Dairy Research Institute (NDRI) on lease. Sardar Patel agreed, and after navigating some bureaucratic red tape, part of the dairy, along with some of its antiquated machines, was rented out to the Kaira Cooperative Union for a sum of Rs. 9,000 a year. The rest of the dairy remained with the NDRI, and became the research creamery where Kurien was to work later as a dairy engineer.

The dairy was old and, as Kurien was to describe it later, fitted with 'a curious assortment of ancient machines'. There was 'a boiler, which, when the pressure was built up, would start a steam engine which would then drive a shaft across the length of the dairy, painfully working the ancient mechanism. There were all kinds of pulleys and belts and pumps. All very impractical, antiquated stuff.' The farmers struggled to get the machines working, with little success.

Tribhuvandas Patel reached out for help to the young, foreign-educated dairy engineer who had recently joined the government research creamery next door. This young engineer was, of course, Verghese Kurien. With very little to do in his own job, and more than a little spare time on his hands, Kurien was glad to help, and would go over to the dairy and fix the machines for them. This was the beginning of the lifelong association between Verghese Kurien and Tribhuvandas Patel that was to change the face of dairying in India.

## CHAPTER FOUR

# 'A PROPHECY THAT CAME TRUE'

SOON BECAME A MATTER OF OUTINE FOR KURIEN TO STEP CROSS AND REPAIR THE ACHINES FOR THE DAIRY ARMERS.
TILL ONE DAY...
CRAP THIS DAIRY. WITH THIS ANTIQUATED EQUIPMENT, YOU WILL EVER MAKE A SUCCESS OF THIS BUSINESS.
I CAN HELP YOU FIX IT, BUT THIS IS NO WAY TO RUN YOUR MILK COOPERATIVE.
WHY DON'T YOU BORROW SOME MONEY AND BUY MODERN DAIRY PLANT EQUIPMENT ?
RIBHUVANDAS DID EXACTLY HAT. HE BORROWED 40,000 UPEES FROM HIS BROTHER IN AW...
AND WITH KURIEN'S HELP ORDERED AND BOUGHT MODERN MACHINERY FOR THE DAIRY.
MEANWHILE KURIEN, COMPLETELY FED UP WITH HIS JOB AT THE GOVERNMENT RESEARCH CREAMERY, CONTINUED TO WRITE TO THE MINISTRY OF AGRICULTURE.
Please relieve me of my current position here at the ...
CLACK CLACK

It was at this time that a curious incident took place in Kurien's life. His friend, Pheroze Medora, was now employed as a chemist by the BMS at their laboratory in Anand. One day, he asked Kurien to go with him to Cambay, where his brother wanted to consult a *chhaya jyotishi*, or 'shadow astrologer'. The jyotishi claimed he could predict a person's future by 'reading' his shadow.

Though Kurien did not believe in such practices, he went along with Medora and his brother. Once the jyotishi had finished with Medora's brother, the others persuaded Kurien to let him read his shadow as well. Kurien gave in, more for the fun of it than any other reason. After declaring that Kurien had no faith, the jyotishi made his calculations and pronounced, 'You are very unhappy in your job right now but within a month you will change it and then you should just sit back and watch. Your career is set for a phenomenal rise—the kind you can never imagine.' Of course, Kurien did not believe him. What could possibly happen to make things better, stuck as he was in the dusty, sleepy, boring little town of Anand?

The jyotishi's predictions were to come eerily true. The Ministry of Agriculture finally accepted Kurien's resignation and released him from his job at Anand. Kurien greeted his release with joy, believing that at last he could get away from Anand and start living again. But just when he was ready to leave …

*Tribhuvandas Patel arrived at my garage door. 'I hear you are leaving,' he said. 'Have you found another job?' I told him I had not but I was going to Bombay to look for one.*

*'In that case, why don't you stay here till you get another job?' he asked. 'You convinced us to order all this expensive equipment which is coming in next week and now you are leaving us in the lurch. None of us here know how to erect all those fancy machines. Why don't you stay here, set up the equipment, get it working, teach our people how to run it and then go?'*

Kurien held Tribhuvandas in high regard, and could not refuse him. He agreed to stay on for two months on a salary of Rs. 600 a month, little realising that at that moment he had found his life's work.

Tribhuvandas Patel was a man of vision and totally dedicated to the well-being of the farmers. His uncompromising integrity made sure that no political or other vested interests could influence his decisions, or the workings of the Kaira cooperatives. Working with him, Kurien learnt an important life lesson—he saw 'that when you work merely for your own profit, the pleasure is transitory; but if you work for others, there is a deeper sense of fulfilment and if things are handled well, the money, too, is adequate'.

Tribhuvandas recognised the need for professionals to run and manage the dairy for the farmers, and finally convinced Kurien to stay on in Anand. In 1950, Kurien formally joined the KDCMPUL as General Manager.

In 1950, dairying in India faced some unique challenges. While most of the world consumes cow's milk, India consumes buffalo milk, and buffaloes give twice the milk in winter than they do in summer. Dairies around the world usually deal with the problem of surplus milk by turning it into milk powder, and turning that back into milk when there is a shortage. But in the early days, the Kaira milk cooperatives did not have the equipment required to make milk powder and therefore had no option except to send all the milk that was produced to Bombay, or else it would spoil and be wasted. By that time, Dara Khurody had become the milk commissioner of Bombay, and he insisted that the Kaira cooperatives send the same amount of milk to Bombay through the year. Rather than taking the surplus milk from Anand, Khurody preferred to import milk powder from New Zealand. Since there was enough liquid milk being produced within the country, Kurien considered this practice both unnecessary and unfair to the farmers. Despite several protests to Khurody, and even complaints to the Government of India, Kurien was unable to stop the import of milk powder from New Zealand.

Meanwhile, milk collection by the Kaira

Cooperatives Union continued to grow, from 200 litres in 1948 to 20,000 litres in 1952. The KDCMPUL was now five years old. The demand for milk from Bombay was also increasing, and insulated railway vans were now being used to transport pasteurised milk from Anand to Bombay. It was evident that a new dairy would soon be needed, with its own railway siding to make the transportation of milk easier and faster.

It was at this juncture that, once again, Kurien was sent abroad by the Government of India to increase his skills and knowledge of dairying.

This time Kurien spent five months in Australia and New Zealand, watching and learning how the then biggest and most modern dairy industry in the world worked. Most importantly, he learnt about the manufacture of milk powder from cow's milk—and came back home to India to organise its production on a commercial scale from buffalo's milk.

Kurien returned to India in April 1953, full of plans for a new dairy and the production of milk powder from buffalo milk. But before he could settle back into work, he received a call from his older brother—he was to go to their mother's home in Trichur, to meet the young woman the family had chosen for him to marry! Kurien, dead against the practice of arranged marriages, had so far resisted all his mother's attempts to get him married. But this time, he was given no option. Besides, said his brother, the young lady would not wait interminably for him. Kurien gave in to his family's demands and set off for Trichur in May 1953, convinced that he would return to Anand still unmarried. Instead, it was love at first sight. The wedding took place within fifteen days, and Kurien returned to Anand from that trip, a married man.

The young woman who had stolen his heart was Susan Molly Peter, or Molly as she was called. Her father was a doctor, as Kurien's had been. Both men had once been students together, and as a result the families were very close. But Kurien and Molly had never met each other before that trip of his to Trichur.

The wedding took place in such a hurry that Kurien had no time to inform his friends and colleagues in Anand. So there was no one at the station to welcome the new bride, and Kurien and Molly simply picked up their cases and walked home.

By this time, Kurien had moved out of the garage into a small house that consisted of a bedroom, a drawing room, a kitchen, and a guest room. All the same, those early years of marriage could not have been easy for Molly. Kurien threw himself into work as soon as they arrived back in Anand, and Molly had to more or less find her own way in a new and alien world, which she did with poise and grace.

While Molly settled into her new life, Kurien became engrossed in his plans for a new dairy and his project to manufacture milk powder out of buffalo milk.

# CHAPTER FIVE
# 'MILK POWDER'

It was now that Harichand Dalaya, Kurien's friend from Michigan State, stepped into the story of the Kaira cooperatives. Dalaya came from a long line of dairymen, and his family had owned a large dairy with three hundred cows in Karachi. The dairy had to be shut down, and Dalaya had been forced to leave for India at Partition. Dalaya was also an excellent dairy technologist, and after his move to India, Kurien persuaded him to join him in Anand.

Tribhuvandas, Kurien and Dalaya became known as the Kaira 'triumvirate'. The three brought different skills to the table, and complemented and completed each other. Tribhuvandas understood the farmers, but recognised that he needed the professional skills of men like Kurien and Dalaya to make the cooperatives work. He was one of the most important political leaders in Gujarat, but never allowed politics to interfere in the workings of the cooperatives, giving Kurien and Dalaya complete trust and the support and freedom to do their job as efficiently as they could. Dalaya was the dairying expert, who understood the methods and technologies of modern dairying, and who could put them in place creatively and innovatively for the Kaira cooperatives. And Kurien was the man at the front, whose job it became to talk to the politicians, the government, and the foreign experts who were soon to become increasingly involved and interested in the Kaira cooperatives.

The three men shared a common vision, and worked together to fulfill it, never allowing their personal disagreements to interfere. Perhaps it was this unique mix of skills and understanding at the top that made the Kaira cooperatives a phenomenon in the dairy industry, not just in India, but very soon, around the world.

UNICEF had agreed to donate dairy equipment for making milk powder to the Kaira Cooperative Union, but for the project to go ahead, approval was needed from the milk commissioner of Bombay. When Khurody heard of the offer, he confidently declared that powder could not be made from buffalo milk; he was supported in his statement by technical experts from England and New Zealand. The government research creamery at Anand in which Kurien had worked as a dairy engineer was already producing powder from buffalo milk, but on a very small scale. Kurien and Dalaya took up the challenge to convince the experts that it could be done.

They arranged for a demonstration at the factory of Teddington Chemicals, a British laboratory company in Andheri, Bombay. They invited Khurody, as well as Dinkarrao Desai, the then Minister in charge of dairying, and the UNICEF representatives, Donald Sabin and T. Glen Davies. Kurien asked Khurody to arrange for some skimmed buffalo milk for the demonstration. Khurody agreed.

The demonstration and its outcome can best be described in Kurien's own words, as he wrote them in his autobiography:

*The next day we met at the Andheri laboratory where Dalaya and I proceeded to convert the buffalo milk into milk powder. Khurody was still sceptical. 'But what about its solubility?' he demanded. I was prepared for this question. I simply added the milk powder to a beaker of distilled water and it dissolved completely. 'But what about its taste?' Khurody persisted. I promptly offered the reconstituted milk to Dinkarrao Desai who sipped it and said it tasted absolutely fine.*

*'It has now been proved that milk powder can be made from buffalo milk. UNICEF will assist Kaira Union to set up the powder plant,' an excited Sabin announced.*

*'But …' began Khurody, trying to introduce yet another doubt.*

*'No more "buts" please,' Davies said, cutting him short. Then pointing to Dalaya and me he remarked, 'I like the cut of the faces of these two young lads and we are, indeed, going ahead with the proposal.'*

*The Bombay state government finally approved the project. Dalaya and I returned victorious to Anand.*

It was only later that Dalaya told Kurien that they had been lucky that Khurody had not known too much about the technical aspects of producing milk powder. Producing powder from skimmed buffalo milk was no different from producing it from skimmed cow's milk. The problem would arise with unskimmed milk that could curdle. But, reassured Dalaya, that was a problem that could be solved by adjusting the level of salts in the unskimmed milk.

After a few hiccups, the machinery finally arrived from UNICEF. Also, Kurien learnt that Khurody had got some land for a government dairy in Anand; after protracted discussions with Dinkarrao Desai, he managed to get this land for the Kaira Cooperative Union's new dairy.

With everything finally in place, Kurien and the others decided to invite Dr Rajendra Prasad, the President of India, to lay the foundation stone for the dairy. The President arrived in Anand, and was taken to the site of the new dairy. As he bent to lay the first foundation stone in the earth, a mouse appeared out of nowhere and jumped over the stone. This was greeted with amazement and cries of joy—for a mouse is the steed of Ganesh, the Hindu god of beginnings, and is therefore considered a very auspicious sign. It was November 15, 1954.

The building of the new dairy and the installation of the new milk powder manufacturing plant were of immense significance. In Kurien's words, 'for the first time in the history of the nation, farmers would actually own the country's most technologically advanced dairy,' upon the functioning of which depended the realisation of their dreams. The blessings of Lord Ganesh were appropriate for a project of such importance.

The date for inaugurating the completed dairy was fixed for October 31,Sardar Patel's birthday, the following year. Completing a project of this magnitude in eleven months had never been done before, and was ambitious even for Kurien and Dalaya. What's more, Sardar Patel's daughter, Maniben, who was a close friend of the Kuriens, had persuaded India's Prime Minister, Jawaharlal Nehru, to inaugurate the dairy. Kurien was nervous, but Dalaya was confident that they would have the dairy and the milk powder plant up and running in time.

Of course, the project faced a host of problems, including a stationmaster who demanded 'payment' for his cooperation in dealing with the wagonloads of construction material that arrived every day for the building site, and the collapse of the boiler room roof while under construction, burying several workers under a huge pile of wet concrete. The stationmaster was quickly and tactfully dealt with by the District Magistrate, and, thanks to swift action by Kurien, who himself pulled out the collapsed beam with a bulldozer before the concrete could solidify, no worker was seriously injured in the boiler room collapse.

The plant was ready just in time—the first batch of milk powder was manufactured in a trial run late at night with only four hours to go for the scheduled inauguration by the Prime Minister the following morning. As Kurien described the moment: 'So thrilled were we with the success that all of us indulged in a spontaneous milk-powder fight!'

Morarji Desai, who was now Chief Minister of Bombay state, had come down to Anand for the inauguration. Khurody, sceptical as always, had told him that no one had built and commissioned a powder plant in one year. What if the plant was not ready for the Prime Minister's visit, worried Morarjibhai. Kurien assured him that it would be, but, as Kurien writes: *'Just in case Khurody is right? What will you do then?' countered a worried Morarjibhai.*

*'Sir, finally what is to be shown to the PM is powder rolling out of the hopper,' I said. 'If need be, some bags of milk powder will be kept on the next floor and fed into the hopper from an inlet upstairs, even as the PM is being shown around.'*

*Morarjibhai quietly walked away. His silence was a consent to the little trick we had up our sleeves, should it prove necessary'.*

UT NO SUCH DECEIT WAS NECESSARY...

... AND, AS JAWAHARLAL NEHRU AND HIS DAUGHTER, INDIRA GANDHI, WERE LED AROUND THE PLANT...

... THE MACHINES WORKED WITHOUT A HITCH, MANUFACTURING MILK POWDER FROM BUFFALO MILK.

S NEHRU LEFT THE PLANT, ORARJI DESAI SAID TO HIM,
MR. KURIEN HAS NOT JUST BUILT AND COMMISSIONED THIS DAIRY IN RECORD TIME,

BUT THIS IS THE FIRST MILK POWDER PLANT IN THE WORLD THAT MAKES MILK POWDER FROM BUFFALO MILK.

KURIEN...

I'M SO GLAD THAT OUR COUNTRY HAS PEOPLE LIKE YOU...

... PEOPLE WHO WILL GO AHEAD AND ACHIEVE EVEN THAT WHICH SEEMS UNACHIEVABLE.

KURIEN NEVER FORGOT THESE WORDS, AND TREASURED THEM ALL HIS LIFE.

It was soon after, that on one of his morning walks around the dairy, Kurien surprised one of the old employees having a drink of milk from one of the cans. The employee was shaken and afraid; Kurien did not say a word, and silently walked away. But the very next day, he told the manager that every employee had to be given half a litre of milk, for, as he explained later, 'these men are handling vast quantities of milk all day long and they are hungry. It is not fair that they do not have a share of the milk.'

And a few years later, in 1962, when a war with China loomed on the horizon, it was to Kurien and the Kaira Cooperatives that the Indian Army turned for help. The army needed milk powder for its soldiers, and Kurien promised to meet its requirements - 2,750 tonnes.

Sardar Patel's vision for the dairy farmers of Kaira had finally come true—the Kaira Cooperative dairy was the largest in all of Asia, and it was owned not by private interest or even the state, but by the farmers themselves. This was an unprecedented and, by all standards, significant achievement for India.

# CHAPTER SIX

# 'UTTERLY, BUTTERLY, DELICIOUS-AMUL'

The KDCMPUL had begun with liquid milk, and with the new dairy and powder plant, it had gone into milk powder. The next product that it now looked at was butter.

Meanwhile, Kurien's wife's brother-in-law, K.M. Philip, who ran his own company, urged Kurien to start marketing the Kaira Cooperative's products, and introduced Kurien to the ideas of branding and advertising. The very first step, of course, was to choose a brand name for their products. After some intense brainstorming in Anand, one of the chemists suggested "Amul". This was met with unanimous approval—the word was derived from the Sanskrit word *amulya*, which meant 'priceless', and therefore effectively conveyed the ideas and ideals behind the Kaira Cooperatives. It could also stand for Anand Milk Union Limited, and was easier on the eye and the ear than the rather clumsy KDMCPUL. And so, in 1957, the Kaira Cooperative Union registered the brand name 'Amul'.

The year 1957 also brought the arrival of a daughter to Verghese and Molly Kurien. They named her Nirmala. She was her father's pride and joy, though, constantly pulled away by work, he could not spend as much time with her as he wanted.

The first product to be branded was butter, and Press Syndicate, an Indian agency, was chosen to handle the advertising campaign. Tribhuvandas was reluctant to spend money on advertising, especially the vast sum of Rs. 2 lakhs that was required, but gave in when Kurien insisted. Jit Kantawala, who looked after the Amul butter ads, managed to give Amul the image of a reliable product that the consumer could trust completely. But it was not till 1966 that the brand came into its own: Amul approached the advertising agency Advertising and Sales Promotion (ASP) to create a new campaign for its butter, with the brief to replace Polson as the leading brand in Bombay. At that time, Sylvester da Cunha was the Managing Director of ASP, and Eustace Fernandez the Art Director. Together, they created an ad campaign that became part of India's psyche, and has gone down in the Guinness Book of World Records as the longest-running ad campaign ever.

Eustace Fernandez created the Amul mascot, the now iconic, round-faced, little girl in a red and white polka dotted dress, and the very first hoarding that said: 'Give us this day our daily bread with Amul Butter'. It also had the tag line, 'utterly, butterly, delicious', a phrase that has become synonymous with Amul butter.

Within a year, the Amul ads took on a topical tone, so that the little Amul moppet began to play the role of social observer. Her witty, perceptive and tongue-in-cheek comments on current affairs were eagerly looked for by consumers—and still are, almost fifty years later. The Amul moppet soon pushed her rival, the Polson butter-girl, off the hoardings, and the advent of Amul butter heralded the end of Polson.

The first few years of production were not easy as Amul butter ran into several unforeseen problems. Polson made its butter from cream supplied by cream merchants. This cream would often be stored for as long as ten days without refrigeration before being turned into butter. The cream would therefore become rancid and stale, and acquire a nasty smell. Before turning it into butter, Polson would put the cream through a vacreator—a machine that would heat the cream very quickly for pasteurisation by injecting it with steam. At the same time, the vacreator would also create a vacuum that would remove the injected steam, rather than allowing it to condense and dilute the cream. The vacreator would also remove most, though not all, of the bad smell, so that the butter made from the cream would retain a certain pungency of flavour and fragrance.

Amul, on the other hand, used only fresh cream and with the result, its butter did not have the sharp flavour of Polson's. Unfortunately, consumers were used to the taste of Polson's, and found Amul butter flat and flavourless. Amul solved this problem by adding diacetyl, a permitted chemical additive, to its butter. This chemical gave the butter the added flavour that the consumers demanded, and the sales of Amul butter increased dramatically.

Another problem was that of colour. The butter from New Zealand was yellow because their cows always ate green grass, which gives a yellow tinge to the milk. Amul used buffalo milk, which is absolutely white, as is the butter made from it. The Indian consumer did not want white butter, so, to please the market, Amul had to add colour to its butter.

Most important for Amul was the question of quality. Despite the need for modifications to their butter to satisfy their consumers, it was also necessary to give them a quality product at an affordable price. This meant further juggling of factors such as the salt and moisture content of the butter—till finally a product was arrived at that satisfied both the perfectionists at Amul and their customers.

Meanwhile, Pestonji, though convinced that a farmers' cooperative could never successfully make butter, was watching Amul with growing concern. Pestonji's methods were old-fashioned, to the extent that he would decide the price of Polson's butter as a daily exercise, depending on the price at which the cream merchants supplied the cream to him each day. Amul, on the other hand, was selling its butter at a steady price that did not vary on a daily basis. This upset Pestonji greatly. He was convinced that this was not the way to do business, and genuinely tried to make Kurien 'see some sense'.

ESTONJI HAD TWO DAIRIES, ONE
N PATNA AND ONE IN ANAND.
POLSON
MODEL DAIRY

HIS ANAND DAIRY WAS MANAGED BY R.H.VARIAVA...

...WHO HAD BECOME A CLOSE FRIEND OF KURIEN'S.

HEN THE KAIRA COOPERATIVE
NION BUILT ITS NEW DAIRY...

VARIAVA PERSUADED PESTONJI TO VISIT THE DAIRY.

HE WAS ASTONISHED BY WHAT HE SAW.

ND AS HE WAS LEAVING.
KURIEN...

MAY KHUDA BLESS YOU FOR ALL THAT YOU HAVE DONE HERE.

HIS WORDS TOUCHED KURIEN DEEPLY.

Despite the fact that Amul and Polson were business rivals, Kurien held Pestonji in great respect. In Kurien's words, 'the unwritten rule at the Kaira Cooperative was to leave him alone. We simply allowed him to do his dairy business his way and we did ours our way.' They had agreed that they would never force him out. Pestonji's business died on its own when it could not face the competition from Amul butter.

Pestonji himself died in November 1962. His son, Minoo, took over the business, and, unable to manage it, finally sold the dairy in Anand to a Marwari businessman who had no interest in the dairy and had bought it only for its land value. The new owner's first act was to have the bust of Pestonji at the entrance thrown out. Variava called up Pestonji's son-in-law, Lt Col Kothawala (who had managed the Anand dairy for a short while after Pestonji's death and before it was sold). Kothawala phoned Kurien, requesting him to save his father-in-law's bust from being disgraced. Kurien promised, and Pestonji's bust was placed in the library of the National Dairy Development Board, 'as a reminder to all of the role that Pestonji Edulji played in the history of Indian dairying'.

Kaira Cooperative now proceeded to expand its operations, and, by the early 1960s, Amul had an established presence in the market not only for milk powder and butter, but also for condensed milk, cheese and baby food. Once again, this did not happen without a struggle, for the farmers' cooperative now had to battle another formidable enemy—the multinational corporation.

In the 1950s and 1960s, the Government of India encouraged investment by foreign companies in India in a limited way. The reasoning behind such encouragement was the hope that multinationals would bring with them newer technology, increase industrial infrastructure and help create a more competitive market structure. Unfortunately, this did not always happen, and the multinationals were often ruthless in their exploitation of the Indian people and the country's resources.

Now, the Swiss multinational, Nestlé, had been given a licence in India to produce condensed milk using Indian milk. Nestlé had, so far, been importing milk powder to manufacture the condensed milk. They had also been importing sugar, and tin plate to make the cans. The Government of India did not approve of this, and in 1956, sent Kurien to Nestlé's headquarters in Switzerland to discuss the situation.

Nestlé's Managing Director, Kreeber, excused their imports of milk powder on the grounds that it was not possible to make condensed milk from buffalo's milk, which is what was available in India. Kurien assured them that while it may be more difficult, it was not impossible to do so, and offered to teach them how. After more discussion, Nestle finally agreed to set up a plant in India. Kurien pointed out that while the plant could start with foreign experts, the Government of India expected them to be replaced with Indians within five years. Kreeber refused, stating that a process as delicate as making condensed milk could not be entrusted to 'the natives'.

Kurien lost his temper at this arrogance and walked out of Nestlé's office, turning down their proposal. Returning to India, he reported the incident to Manubhai Shah, who was then the Industries and Commerce Minister for the Government of India—and suggested that Amul start manufacturing condensed milk instead. The Minister agreed.

Two years later, Amul's condensed milk was in the market, and Kurien asked the government to ban the import of condensed milk. The government did so, effectively shutting out Nestlé. A few weeks later, Manubhai Shah rang Kurien with the news that Nestlé was now keen to set up a plant in India, but that he had refused to see their representatives unless they had a letter of introduction from Kurien! It was to be Kurien's decision whether Amul could meet the demand for condensed milk in India on its own, or whether Nestlé would be allowed entry into the country.

Kurien agreed to meet the Nestlé representatives—there were four of them, including Kreeber. When they arrived in Anand, Kurien suggested that they pay a visit to their condensed milk plant before they sat down for discussions. They did so, and when they returned, Kurien turned to Kreeber and asked, 'Well, Mr. Kreeber, what do you think of the "natives" now?'

Kreeber, deeply embarrassed, apologised humbly and sincerely to Kurien, both for his own behaviour and on behalf of his firm. 'We want to participate in India's dairy development and we will do it only according to the rules you may lay down,' he said.

Kurien gave them the letter of introduction, and Nestlé became a big player in the Indian market. But even as Kurien gave the letter, he had his reservations. Though he was not against foreign investment in India, he believed that it should be allowed only on India's terms, in areas where either technology or capital was lacking, and in a manner that would help, rather than further exploit, the country. However, once multinationals gained entry, it became difficult to control them. The only way to contain exploitation by multinationals, he believed, was to produce cheaper and better products than they did, as Amul proceeded to do with their baby food.

Amul's main competitor in the baby food market was the multinational firm, Glaxo. Glaxo's baby food was securely established, and Amul knew it had a hard battle ahead. As a first step, a great deal of care was taken to formulate the baby food, and, once again, it was Harichand Dalaya who came up with the final formula. Amul would use its own milk powder, and fortify it with vitamins.

The next challenge was to convince the Indian consumer to buy their product, and Amul launched an advertising campaign. This was greeted with huge protests, as activist groups objected to the advertising of baby food as unethical and promoting unhealthy practices since it discouraged the breastfeeding of babies. But Amul was ready for these attacks, and brought out an Amul Baby Book that emphasised the superiority of mother's milk over artificially-formulated baby food. Amul also spent time and money educating mothers on nutrition. They were also the first to realise that milk lacked Vitamin A, and so added Vitamin A to their baby food, along with Vitamin D that helps absorb Vitamin A. And of course, the consumer had to be convinced that baby food made from buffalo milk was as good as that made from cow's milk! But Amul won the battle and finally displaced Glaxo as the most preferred brand of baby food in the market.

# CHAPTER SEVEN
# 'THE ANAND MODEL'

The Kaira Cooperative Union grew from strength to strength, and very soon, the Kaira district's model of dairy farming was adopted in the five neighbouring districts of Mehsana, Banaskantha, Baroda, Sabarkantha and Surat, and District cooperative unions similar to the Kaira Cooperative Union were formed in each district. An apex body to market the produce of these unions was set up in 1973; this was the Gujarat Cooperative Milk Marketing Federation Limited (GCMMF). The creation of the GCMMF at the top completed what has come to be known as the 'Anand pattern' of dairy development, a model that was replicated with tremendous success across India, and which has become the model for dairy farming across the developing world.

The success of the 'Anand model' of dairy cooperatives lies in its strongly democratic structure, which involves the dairy farmers at every level. It begins at the village—a cooperative milk society is created in each village by the dairy farmers, who become members of that cooperative. They then elect a managing committee from amongst themselves, and one of the elected members of the committee is chosen to be the chairman. The chairmen of these managing committees form the district cooperative union, and elect from amongst themselves a board of directors. The cooperative union owns the dairy plant, and its board of directors guides and oversees the management of the district union and the running of the dairy plant.

In the same way that village cooperatives are represented at the district level through the district cooperative union, the district cooperative unions are further represented at the state level through the state cooperative milk marketing federation. This body helps in the marketing of the liquid milk and milk products produced by the district cooperative unions. It brings the products directly to the consumers, eliminating all middlemen between the milk producers and their consumers.

This three-tiered structure—at village, district, and state levels—with each tier responsible to the one below, is a distinguishing feature of the Anand model of dairy cooperatives. Thus the state federation is responsible to the district unions, and the district unions to the village cooperatives, which are responsible to their members, the dairy farmers. This structure ensures that production, as well as distribution, marketing and sales of milk and milk products, remains in the hands of the dairy farmers.

Very early on, Tribhuvandas Patel recognised that the farmers needed to employ men like Verghese Kurien and Harichand Dalaya to manage and run their business, for they had skills that the farmers did not have.

KURIEN TOO BELIEVED FIRMLY IN THE NEED FOR PROFESSIONAL MANAGERS.

Soon after, upon the suggestion of Ravi Matthai, Kurien began work on building his own school for training professional managers. He asked Ravi Matthai to join him, and together the two men created IRMA, the Institute of Rural Management at Anand, which opened its doors to students in 1979. Ravi Matthai had also been the man behind the creation of IIM-A, and he brought his great experience and wisdom to bear on the creation of IRMA. Unfortunately, Ravi Matthai died before IRMA was complete. The library at the institute was named the Ravi Matthai Library in his memory.

The employment by the cooperative unions of such professional managers and technologists to run and operate their business remains another distinguishing feature of the Anand model of dairy cooperatives.

Tribhuvandas Patel started the dairy cooperatives movement in Kaira in 1946, as a protest against the practices of the British government. He began with two village cooperatives, collecting some 200 litres of milk a day. By 2005, there were 1,017 village cooperatives in Kaira, with 5,73,962 dairy farmers as their members, collecting 7,39,000 litres of milk a day. Today, this district cooperative alone earns more than Rs. 4,000 million a year as profits through the sale of its milk and milk products. The more the farmers produce, the greater their profits, and the more each farmer gets in return.

The dairy cooperative movement in Kaira not only increased farm incomes, it also brought about a social revolution in the villages, breaking barriers of gender, caste and class. For example, the queues at the milk collection centres were strictly on a first-come first-served basis—those farmers who came first would be attended to first. No longer could a Brahmin demand that his milk be collected before that of a harijan. And what was even more revolutionary, the milk from a higher caste farmer was treated in exactly the same way as the milk from a harijan. The milk from both farmers flowed into the same can, and was bought and sold as the same product. There was no longer any distinction of caste. In the same way, men could not demand to be served before women. Social and economic divisions were further weakened by the democratic structure of the cooperatives, which made sure that the most competent, rather than the rich or high caste, were chosen to run them.

Another very important outcome of this movement was the empowerment of village women as the dairy cooperatives put income directly into the hands of the farmer's wife. The cooperatives gave the women not only a fair price for their milk, but as the dairy business grew and became more profitable, it also gave them more income, so that often a woman's income became equal to that of her husband's. As the woman's income increased, so did her standing in the family—she now had a say in how the family money, and in particular, her income, was to be spent. This resulted in additional benefits such as better nutrition and health for herself and her children.

The dairies brought modern technology and organisation to the village, and often served as a model for improvement in other aspects of the farmers' lives. For example, to keep the milk pure and free of contamination, it was necessary that the dairies were kept clean and free of flies and rats, and that vessels were washed and sterilised. This insistence on cleanliness taught the farmers the importance of hygiene and sanitation.

The Kaira Union also employed a team of fifteen veterinarians who would visit every village once in two weeks, treating sick animals free of charge. These vets provided much-needed care for the animals, saving cattle from disease and other problems that might once have killed them. A farmer could phone the cooperative and ask for the vet—who would be available all the time, any day of the week. Efficient and effective healthcare for the animals made the farmers seek better care for themselves as well, so that the Kaira Union began healthcare programmes, especially for women and children.

The farmers were also encouraged to visit the cattle-feed plants, and the artificial insemination centres. Discussions on appropriate nutrition for their animals led the women to consider questions of nutrition for themselves and their children, and, as they understood the processes of contraception and birth in their cattle, they began to relate these issues to themselves. In the wake of this awareness, there came a steadily-growing improvement in women and child health.

Thus the dairy cooperative movement gradually became a movement for social growth and change, and improved the life of hundreds of thousands of rural men, women and children.

In 1964, the Kaira Union set up a new cattle-feed factory at Kanjari, a few kilometres from Anand. They decided to invite the then Prime Minister of India, Lal Bahadur Shastri, to inaugurate the plant. Shastriji accepted the invitation, but he added that he would like to spend a night in a village in Kaira district, as the guest of a small farmer. This unusual request caused a great deal of concern and anxiety regarding the Prime Minister's safety and security, but ultimately Kurien and the Home Secretary, F.J. Heredia, were able to work out a plan to satisfy Shastriji's request.

The Prime Minister spent the night in the

village of Ajarpura, a few kilometres from Anand, as the guest of a small farmer, Ramanbhai Patel. He talked to the villagers for a long time, questioning them at length about their lives and the problems they faced. He also asked about the dairy cooperative in their village and its impact upon them. The next morning he visited the village milk cooperative, where Kurien met him and explained its working to him. Finally, Shastriji reached Anand. After inaugurating the cattle-feed plant, he returned with Kurien to the latter's house.

The Prime Minister questioned Kurien closely about the reasons for the success of Anand and Amul. 'We have built so many dairies across India,' said the Prime Minister, 'but with the exception of Amul, all are unmitigated disasters, running at a loss … I want to know why this particular dairy is a success when all others have failed.' And that is why, explained Shastriji, he had spent a night talking to the farmers, trying to understand the reasons for Amul's success. But he had been unable to find a single reason why Amul should have succeeded while the other dairies had failed. There was nothing special about Kaira district—the soil was average, the climate like most of the rest of India, as was the rainfall. The buffaloes in Gujarat were not as good or as high-yielding as the buffaloes in Uttar Pradesh. The farmers were hard-working, but not as hard-working as the farmers of Punjab. 'I can't find a single reason why Anand is such a great success. Now can you please tell me what is the secret of its success?'

Kurien assured the Prime Minister that he was right, that there was no difference between Amul and the other cooperatives—except one. This single and vital difference was that the Amul dairy was owned by the farmers themselves. The farmers elected representatives from amongst themselves to manage the dairy; these representatives in turn employed professional managers like himself to run their dairy.

Shastriji listened to Kurien's answer in growing excitement. If the success of Amul was not due to an intrinsic factor like soil or climate, it meant that the story of Amul could be copied across India! Kurien agreed.

'So then, Kurien,' said the Prime Minister, 'from tomorrow you shall make it your business to work not just for Anand, not just for Gujarat, but for the whole of India. The Government of India will give you a blank cheque, it will create any body, any structure you want, provided you will head it. Please replicate Anand throughout India. Make that your mission, and whatever you need for it, the government will provide.'

Kurien had two conditions: first, that he would

remain an employee of the farmers, and not become an employee of the government, for that way he would be free of any pressures the government may seek to apply, and could do his job with only the farmers' interests in mind; second, he would not move to Delhi, but do the job from Anand where he would be closer to the farmers and their concerns.

The Prime Minister agreed to his conditions, and Kurien accepted the work. And so was born the 'billion-litre' idea that led to Operation Flood and the revolution in dairy farming and milk production across India, that ultimately transformed India from a milk-deficit nation into the largest milk producer in the world.

# CHAPTER EIGHT
# 'OPERATION FLOOD'

In order to fulfill his vision of replicating Amul across the country, the Prime Minister decided that a new organisation would be needed, with Kurien at its head. This became the National Dairy Development Board (NDDB), which was set up in 1965, and headquartered at Anand. Despite the NDDB having the Prime Minister's support, the government refused to sanction the funds for its creation, so that finally it was financed by the dairy farmers of Amul—which was perhaps fitting in a way, given its objective. The NDDB adopted as its logo a stylised representation of the Indus Valley bull.

Kurien realised very soon, that rather than expecting the state governments to release funds to set up dairy cooperatives in their state, the NDDB would have to finance the cooperatives itself, and he put together a proposal with the help of his friend Harichand Dalaya and the Food & Agriculture Organisation (FAO) expert Michael Halse. The team finalised their proposal in 1968; they called their proposed project 'Operation Flood'.

In the 1960s and '70s, milk production in India was falling, despite the fact that India had the largest cattle population in the world. An important reason for this was the manner in which milk was supplied to the cities. The practice in India was to transport the best, most high-yielding cattle to the cities every year. The buffaloes would be brought into the city every year as soon as they had calved. The newborn calves would also be brought with their mothers, so that the latter would be encouraged to give milk. Once in the city, the buffaloes would be trained to give milk even without the presence of their calves, and once this had been done, the calves would be slaughtered. The buffaloes themselves would be kept in the most dreadful conditions, and once they stopped giving milk, they too would be killed. These cruel and inefficient practices meant that the country was systematically destroying its best and most high-yielding cattle. In Bombay alone, some 1,00,000 calves were killed every year.

Also, the milk thus provided was low in quality—the vendors would dilute it with water, which was usually impure. They would also charge very high prices for this adulterated milk. The milk schemes in the various cities, which sought to provide milk gathered from the villages, could not meet the demand for milk in the cities, so that the private vendors continued to supply their poor quality milk at extremely high prices.

Operation Flood sought to change this situation by working out solutions so that valuable milch cattle would not need to be taken to the cities, and milk could be collected in rural areas and then transported to the cities, as was being done in Anand. This, Kurien and his colleagues believed, would encourage the growth and development of the dairy industry, help the dairy farmers, and make more milk available across the country—again, benefits that had been proven in Anand.

Their plan was to build four dairies—the Mother Dairies, as we know them today—one for each of India's four metros, Bombay, Delhi, Calcutta and Madras. These dairies were to be served by twenty-seven cooperative dairying areas—which they called milksheds—across ten states. The milksheds were to be organised along the lines of the Anand model. The liquid milk collected by these twenty-seven milksheds would then be transported to the cities. Kurien and his team calculated that this would cost around Rs 6,500 million. They also knew that this money would not be forthcoming either from the state governments or the Government of India.

Now, at just that time, there arose a surplus of milk products in Europe. Kurien saw a unique opportunity here to raise funds for their plan, and together with his team, raised a proposal asking the European Economic Community (EEC) to gift their surplus to the NDDB. Kurien's plan was to sell this surplus in India and use the money thus generated to set up his dairies. His proposal was initially met with much bureaucratic resistance from the Government of India, but after a lot of hard work and harder convincing of government officials by Kurien, it was finally cleared.

The EEC gifted milk powder and butter oil to the NDDB, which sold them at prices comparable to those charged by Indian farmers; these commodities were reconstituted into milk and sold in the metros. Thus Kurien not only raised enough money to finance the dairy cooperatives, but at the same time created a demand for quality milk at reasonable prices in the cities.

Kurien's plan involved three stages. First, the donated surplus from the EEC was to be reconstituted into milk, which was to be supplied to the milk schemes in the four metro cities. This would make sure that the milk schemes could provide enough quality milk to the cities to obtain a larger share of the market from the private vendors. It would also create a demand for good quality milk at reasonable prices. Second, the money raised from the reconstitution and sale of the surplus would be used to set up the four dairies, and to increase the organised production, collection and processing of milk. The city-kept cattle were also to be resettled, so that they could breed, adding to the supply of high-yielding milch cattle in the country. And third, a national milk grid was to be set up, to make sure that all the major cities, and the milk schemes operating with them, were supplied with adequate milk—by rail and road, from villages that could sometimes be 2,000 kms away. These three stages of Operation Flood ultimately were completed over a period of three decades.

Kurien's 'billion-litre idea' was officially put into action by the NDDB in July, 1970. Its goal was 'to take India's dairy industry from a drop to a flood'. Despite delays in implementation and many hiccups along the way, Operation Flood became the biggest dairy development programme in the world, and made India self-sufficient in milk and milk products. By 1975, all imports of milk and milk products had stopped. Milk production increased from 20 million tonnes a year in the 1960s, to 127 million tonnes in 2012. Today, India is the largest milk-producing nation in the world. There are 1,44,246 dairy cooperative societies across the country with more than 15 million dairy farmers as their members. The milk collected by these cooperative societies is processed in 177 district cooperative unions, and marketed by 22 state marketing federations. Some of the more successful state marketing federations, whose products have become familiar household brands, include Verka in Punjab, Vijaya in Andhra Pradesh and Gokul in Maharashtra.

When Operation Flood was five years old, Kurien and his colleagues felt the need to record its progress. Several documentaries giving facts and figures had already been made, including some by the legendary filmmaker Shyam Benegal. It was during a conversation with Kurien that Benegal pointed out that while the documentaries were good, they did not capture the human aspect of Operation Flood. It was then that Kurien suggested that he make a film, telling some of these stories, and Benegal agreed.

As always, there was the issue of money—how would they fund a full-length film on Operation Flood? Kurien's colleagues at Anand suggested that they ask the farmers. Kurien did so—and 5,00,000 dairy farmers, every single member of the Gujarat milk cooperatives, gave Rs 2, so that a million rupees were soon collected and deposited in the bank. Shyam Benegal put together an extremely talented team—playwright Vijay Tendulkar researched the story and wrote it, while the characters in the film were played by some of India's most gifted actors, including Smita Patil, Naseeruddin Shah, Anant Nag and Girish Karnad. It took nine months of shooting in the villages of Gujarat.

THE FILM WAS CALLED MANTHAN, AND WAS RELEASED IN 1976.

GUJARAT CO-OPERATIVE MILK MARKETING FEDERATION LTD

500,000 FARMERS OF GUJARAT
PRESENT

MANTHAN
(THE CHURNING)

# CHAPTER NINE
# 'BOUQUETS AND BRICKBATS'

The success story of Operation Flood spread far and wide, so that soon Kurien was hosting a steady stream of foreign visitors to Anand, including, in March 1979, the Soviet Premier, Alexei Kosygin. Though he was full of praise for Kurien's achievements at Amul, he had one criticism:

*'Dr Kurien,' he said, 'you took thirty years to achieve this in milk—an entire lifetime—and you faced a lot of problems. When you set up the milk cooperatives, nobody really realised what you were up to. If you try to do the same for vegetable oil, where big people are involved, everyone will know. Tomorrow, Dr Kurien, you may think of doing the same for cotton or jute and you will then upset the biggest people in India. Besides, you will take thirty years to do it in vegetable oil and then another thirty years to do the same for cotton and jute. Such significant social and economic changes that you are trying to bring about should not be done in leisurely fashion. These changes should be brought about quickly—in all directions, all at once. It has to be a revolution. For if you do it slowly, Dr Kurien, you will be shot down like a dog.'*

KOSYGIN INVITED KURIEN TO RUSSIA TO SEE THE EFFECT OF THEIR REVOLUTION FOR HIMSELF.
INSTRUCTED BY THE GOVERNMENT OF INDIA TO DO SO, KURIEN ACCEPTED HIS INVITATION.
HE CAME BACK LESS THAN IMPRESSED BY SOVIET RUSSIA, AND BY THE STATE OF THEIR DAIRY INDUSTRY.
THE CATTLE WERE IN BAD SHAPE. THE COWS WERE OWNED COLLECTIVELY AND SINCE THEY BELONGED TO THE STATE...
" IT MEANT THAT NOBODY OWNED THEM AND THEREFORE NOBODY TOOK CARE OF THEM. "
" SIMILARLY, THE DAIRIES TOO WERE OWNED BY THE STATE AND THEIR CONDITION WAS DISMAL.
KOSYGIN'S ADVICE WAS INCORRECT.
CHANGE MUST TAKE TIME AND THE MORE CAREFULLY IT WAS BROUGHT ABOUT...
THE MORE PERMANENT IT WOULD BE.

Countries across Asia, Africa and Latin America continued to be impressed by India's achievements in Operation Flood, and sent officials, experts and farmers to India to understand and learn the Anand pattern. Kurien was invited to both Pakistan and Sri Lanka to help implement the Anand model in those countries. While the political climate in Pakistan prevented the effective implementation of the Anand model there, Sri Lanka set up its Kiriya Milk Industries in collaboration with the NDDB.

In India, the Anand model was also successfully used for other agricultural commodities such as fruit and fresh vegetables. NDDB was also asked by the Government of India to enter the vegetable oils market. The 700-crore project to cooperatise the vegetable oils industry was launched in 1979. By 1986, over 3,00,000 farmers had joined 2,500 Oilseed Growers' Cooperatives across the seven states in which the project had been started, and by 1994, there were 5,348 cooperatives with about a million farmers as their members. Packaged, edible oil sourced from these cooperatives was introduced into the Indian market under the brand name 'Dhara'. This was marketed by the GCMMF, which already had a distribution network of 5,00,000 retail outlets to market Amul. Dhara was an almost instant success, and despite competition from other branded oils sold by multinationals, India’s edible oil import bill came down from Rs. 1,000 crore to Rs. 165 crore.

Of course, implementing the Anand pattern meant that procuring, processing and marketing of vegetable oils was now in the hands of the oilseed farmers. This eliminated the middlemen, the powerful oil kings or telia rajahs. Needless to say, the oil kings did not take kindly to Kurien’s efforts, and did all they could to make it difficult for him.

Kurien had other detractors too. The multinational lobby was directly threatened, and therefore seriously upset by the achievements of Amul and other dairy cooperatives. Nor did all the politicians or bureaucrats in the Government of India look with approval upon Kurien and his methods, and Kurien’s fierce temper, and his blunt and forthright manner, did not exactly smoothen his way. Fortunately for India, Kurien’s tenacity and perseverance, and his complete dedication to the welfare of the Indian farmers, overcame these various challenges.

Kurien had been appointed chairman of the NDDB in 1965, and resigned in 1998. He also resigned as the General Manager of the GCMMF in 1981, though he continued as Honorary Chairman. He was the chairman of the Gujarat Cooperative Milk Marketing Federation for thirty-four years and stepped down in 2006; the GCMMF now has more than three million members.

Despite the success of Amul, cooperative salaries have never matched those of multinationals, so that the highest salary that Kurien ever drew was Rs. 5,000 as the chairman and General Manager of GCMMF. But money was never the driving factor for Kurien, nor for his wife Molly, and they managed contentedly within the salary that Kurien drew. They finally moved into their own house in Anand in 1989, bought from Kurien's savings over the years.

The absence of monetary reward was more than made up for by the many awards and honours that Kurien received. In 1965, his old school, the Michigan State University, conferred on him the honorary degree of Doctor of Science, thereby 'promoting' him, as he put it, 'from an ordinary "Mr. Kurien" to "Dr Kurien".' The first international recognition of his work came in 1963, with the Ramon Magsaysay Award for Community Leadership, which he shared with Tribhuvandas Patel and Dara Khurody. He also received three of India's top civilian honours, the Padma Shri in 1965, the Padma Bhushan in 1966, and the Padma Vibhushan in 1999. Today, the house in Anand that he once lived in with Molly, has been turned into a museum—and on its walls are hung more than a hundred and fifty awards and citations from around the world.

***

Kurien's achievements can only be spoken of in the superlative. His work for dairy development and rural empowerment was phenomenal.

These larger-than-life achievements are enough to make us pause in wonder. But even more than the achievements themselves, we must marvel at the man behind them. As a young man, Kurien stood out amongst his peers for his sharp intelligence. He was also strong-willed, to the point of obstinacy sometimes, a quality which often stood him in good stead as it helped him push through ideas and plans. He did not give up easily, even in the most dismal situations, such as during his initial days in Anand; instead, he turned every challenge into an opportunity. Despite his initial reluctance to get involved with rural India, once he had accepted the challenge, he put aside all thoughts of personal gain or comfort, and worked single-mindedly for the welfare of the farmers. Kurien was not always an easy man to deal with—his fiery temper, his refusal to compromise, and his outspokenness ruffled many feathers during his career. But when it came to the welfare of the farmers, he was patient, dogged in the pursuit of his objectives, and very practical. He was also a man of integrity and unsullied honesty. Most of all, he had a vision, a dream for the farmers of India, and he dedicated his life to make this dream come true.

***

Dr Verghese Kurien, the Milkman of India, passed away on September 9, 2012, after a brief illness in Nadiad, near Anand. He was 90 years old.

His wife, Molly, followed him on December 14, 2012, in Mumbai.

Dr Kurien and his wife are survived by their daughter, Nirmala.

# Acknowledgements

I would first like to thank the family of Dr Verghese Kurien—in particular his daughter, Nirmala Kurien, and his nephew Gautam John—for their help.

I would also like to thank Ms Priya Kapoor of Roli Books, for kindly giving me permission to use Dr Kurien's autobiography, *I Too, Had a Dream*, as told to Gouri Salvi, as a source of reference, and for allowing me to quote freely and fully from it. Dr Kurien's autobiography remains my primary source of information for this book.